Contents

The Chess Game	11
I've been thinking about your birth lately	12
Joint Statement	14
The Drop Off	16
|We're going to get nailed|	32
Disconcerting tendencies	34
recline	35
Cystometrogram	37
The Specimens on Crown Street	39
⁃Intensifier⁃	41
Vision	49
Thumbsucker	52
The Experience Economy	54
seaweed	58
jaffas	59
siege	60
stair/case	61
Sister	62
Kale	63
a dog is not a child	64
Child Support [Calculator]	66

Prime Cuts	68
(Un)found(ed)	71
Year of the Rat	74
Reserves	75
Landlords	76
Review	77
Fifteen ways to be erased	78
Dad/Bingo	88
Grounds for Divorce	90
Game	94
Kill [All The Birds]	97
Montage	99
Notes	103
Acknowledgements	105

Endorsements for *The Drop Off*

David Stavanger writes poems of excruciating beauty, associative insight and acute humanity like no-one else I know. From the complexities of shared parenting to the housing crisis, from the corporatisation of everyday life to the alienations of the medical system, *The Drop Off* lands in the reader's body with devastating and revelatory effect.

Andy Jackson

The Drop Off raises crucial questions about how and why we are blindly complicit in diminishing our lives in ways that threaten to undermine our capacity to value the very qualities that characterise us as human. Amid the heartbreak and melancholy, the unsettled and unsettling, there is much humour, too. These poems are extraordinary animals. Stavanger has an astute and unflinching eye – and a talent for matter-of-factly corralling mundane everyday details to absurd effect.

Grace Yee

Praise for *Case Notes*

Case Notes is a visceral and profound meditation on masculinity, mental illness, fatherhood, family and suburban life.

2021 Victorian Premier's Literary Awards judges

Case Notes is a remarkable work: surreal, poignant, original, astute, and a deftly balanced blend of funny and vulnerable.

Dženana Vucic, Cordite

The Drop Off

David Stavanger

David Stavanger is a poet, producer, parent, and (lapsed) psychologist living on Wodi Wodi Dharawal land. He is the co-editor of *Solid Air: Australian & New Zealand Spoken Word* (UQP, 2019) and *Admissions: Voices Within Mental Health* (Upswell, 2022). His previous collection *Case Notes* (UWAP, 2020) won the 2021 Victorian Premier's Literary Award for Poetry.

David Stavanger

The Drop Off

First published in Australia in 2025
by Upswell Publishing
Perth, Western Australia
upswellpublishing.com

Upswell operates in the city of Perth, on ancient country of the Whadjuk people of the Noongar nation who remain the spiritual and cultural custodians of this beautiful land. We acknowledge their continuing connection to country and express gratitude to elders past and present for their strength and creativity ... Always was, always will be, Aboriginal land.

This book is copyright. Apart from any fair dealing for the purpose of private study, research, criticism or review, as permitted under the *Copyright Act 1968*, no part may be reproduced by any process without written permission. Enquiries should be made to the publisher.

Copyright © 2025 by David Stavanger

The moral right of the author has been asserted.

ISBN: 978-0-645-98408-8

 A catalogue record for this book is available from the National Library of Australia

Cover design by Chil3, Fremantle
Typeset in Foundry Origin by Lasertype
Printed by Lightning Source

Upswell Publishing is assisted by the State of Western Australia through its funding program for arts and culture.

Dedicated to Saul

The Chess Game
In response to Marcel Duchamp's The Chess Game *1910*

My son and I play chess
every morning during his custody visits.
We're willing to sacrifice our queens, putting
them aside for the duration of the exchange.
Sometimes I let him win, sometimes he wins.
We hunch over, contemplating next moves
(he's never glued my pieces to the board).
It's a magnetic set, a masterclass in overcoming
boredom. He's always white. Goes first.

One day we'll play
without consent order
on the outskirts of Paris.

I've been thinking about your birth lately

striving to recall details of how this started,
    the gasp of you under fluorescent light.
        Dreamt up midwives in revolving shifts,
witnessing labour stretch night's thin fray.

And the transitions: canned laughter to small talk
    the switch between active to tableaux of rest,
        dilation of rooms and contraction of sheets.
I can't remember what your face looked like

under the medics' watchful eyes,
    whether you smelt of the hot milk of beginnings.
        Did I bring a change of shirt
for the absence of euphoria, the presence of blood?

Possibly a nurse was discussing the weather,
    beyond the birthing suite the sun had surely risen.
        It is impossible to say if I was in attendance—
no drugs in me, anaesthetised in other ways.

When you were conceived I didn't want to live,
    courting the formation of a darker star.
        I still study your sonogram daily,
this postnatal amnesia a sentence—

I crave the crown of fine hair, the physicality of child.
    To hold a living thing knowing it's as much mine
        as another's, the warm rubber of umbilical cord
thawed calamari tube cut in two for takeaway.

The placenta is the body's only disposable organ,
      though other vital parts of us are expelled after birth.
           I think we put yours in the freezer, to deter predators
and reassure other parents. History likes to record firsts.

The first time I held you close I caught fire.
      Earthdrawn boy, diving reflex engaged to free fall.
           Breaching silence, you knew my taste in music.
Storage boxes foraged for clues, trying to retrieve

your arrival I emerge with connective tissue.
      In that nursery of strange wet babies, considering flight
           from maternity's wing. Monitoring breath's escape,
units of dependency measured in the phrases of a lullaby.

Sometimes I read your certificate as an unofficial record of life.
      I have the DNA. Know the formal date. Still fret when you're late.
           It's hard to say what kind of parents we will become.
There's no way to inoculate against this future heartbreak.

Joint Statement

our careers are of paramount import(ance).
    we will continue to thrive as a conscious product
albeit in a different shape ◆⸝◆ ⎩ ⎧ ■
    we agree to boost co(operations) in the co(parenting) domain.
what remains is a commitment to realise
    a common vision for a free and open-hearted market.
to take the bilateral relationship forward
    we have lovingly chosen sovereign states (much thought).
we get to control the presentation of our love story.
    we adhered to the cultural values of romance norms
now this magical journey together has taken a familiar path.
    we are honoured to have contributed
to the evolution of dissolution.
    no secrets nor salacious events are at the root
if fault is to be assigned, let it be assigned to circumstance.
    we're venturing towards new bright horizons
throwing hidden shade as diplomatic agents.
    the 'd' word in this statement indicates that this is final.
we have commenced the progressive route out of sadness.
    any claims regarding ▮▮▮▮▮▮▮▮▮ are untrue.
however, yes, we have had a rough year.
    before rumours or falsifications get out of hand
we have divested to pursue our individual growth.
    we agree to establish a new horizontal agenda
parting ways is as natural as procreating.
    after a week away of wonderful days
we have mutually resolved to end this transaction amicably.
    while this may not be the 'end', it is the end for now.
we feel compelled to share our post-truth
    in our own way, and within our own timing.

truly this is a united decision
    separate 'I' statements don't indicate animosity.
we would never violate the script
    the words matter less than the fact that we are using them.
it's really hard to hard-launch this divorce
    we request privacy and publicity in equal measures, thanks.

The Drop Off

3.
The modern dilemma.
You unconsciously coupled.
You consciously uncoupled.
In between you had a child
with your combined chromosomes,
threads dividing under microscope.
He was three when things fell apart,
past tense yet to wholly develop.
He was gentle and he was verbal,
a thousand words without estrangement.

You told him late afternoon in a local park
near the military memorial,
unable to fully articulate
the covert ways of war
before it got dark.

4.
Living alone, you no longer let another
adult know that a bath has been drawn.
The temperature of the water adequate,
to cover the lack of warmth in a text
confirming a medical appointment
or the location of an errant toy.

Such objects travel between places
taking notes of dispositions
and the absence of 'our' son,
co-existing as childhood cargo, a constant
reminder from two sets of shelves
that an atom can be split || like a home.

5.
The neutrality of the duck pond.
A point of exchange, a place of breadcrumbs
reviewing consent orders with a blunt pencil.
Children cannot be left unsupervised
near the water's edge, nerve endings exposed
by the emphasis on dot-point accountability.
Document signing on a bench, clenched stale
bread in one hand, broken lead in the other.

It's the best place for children to meet new partners
by picnic and by subterfuge, though opening dips
and spreading out old blankets is not enough
to host the strangeness of complex fractions,
breaking bread without common denominator
beyond the need to find a five-year-old a surfacing turtle,
everything expressed as brightly as winter sunlight.

6.
A child will begin to crave their parents reuniting.
They will express it in the way they linger at a door,
drawings of two crayon faces merged into one,
rapidly stroking your eyebrow with a wet thumb.
Sleep becomes unsettled, moods verge on fragile.
A pair of running shoes is filled with marbles.
I made a wand. We baked an angel cake for you.
The reunification fantasy taking concrete shape.

You were away a lot that year.
You treated your son as an inconvenience.
You disappeared into the idea
you were important.

7.
Shaking up routines escalates tensions.
It's essential to go to the same park straight after pick-up.
Pull up by old figs gathering at the edges
scout the area for other single fathers clutching
takeaway coffee and plastic-wrapped chip sandwiches.
Undo a belt to release your child from an approved booster,
follow them to the boat-themed climbing structure with slide,
then nest swing and attempts to balance on the octopus seesaw.
When your child enters the fort, give them time to strategise
secure in the stronghold of imagination, presiding over toy soldiers.
Next cafe replica, bark pieces exchanged for the currency of a smile.
Closer to the river some families are still together, you walk
over slowly to the spinning puzzles and give them a mighty twirl.

8.
At times there will be a third party present.
They will offer your child gifts,
some wrapped, some that require reciprocation,
bright tokens to cross a bridge of soft bones
built from within another's skin.
There is no way to stop a stranger
unrequitedly loving what you can't relinquish,
that which you cradle and carry alone.
There is too much baggage and not enough of them
visible in the cheeks and gait and interests.

These are days of apprehension and forced relations,
trying to teach a pre-schooler to divide and subtract.
Take crib notes. Survey the lack of laughter in a face
formed in the writers' room of separation and sitcom:
even if you take the managing absence masterclass
the best punchlines rarely involve a single-parent
leaving a child to fend for itself.

9.
Judgement-free zones are rarely free of judgement.
The GP examines you both and frowns
when you don't know a child's exact weight or what they
ate the night before. The school advisor asks how
things are at home and makes notes before you reply.
At a birthday party, you drink wine instead of sparkling
water and the shitbox car you drive is barely roadworthy.
Someone tries to set you up with another struggling mother.
A circus of lucent strangers gathers around sushi and sprinkles,
make most of their kid's food from scratch, endorse up-scaled
early life moments and personalised parenting plans, someone
confides how hard it is to be both a father and a football coach.
Within these conversations, you are smaller than a nuclear family.
You watch your son ask for a balloon animal that doesn't exist.

10.
They move across a border.
They move far south where the mountains
cast long shadows upon the sea.
They move with legal precedent,
move with righteous intent
to the scaffold of extended family.
They move as night wind,
leaving the sun's skin behind
taking everything except overripe
mangoes fallen at the front door,
rotting in the stillness that follows.

Conceding literal ground at mediation,
the tyrant of pride overcome by the sound
of impermanent marker drawing up percentage
of care on whiteboard, the detritus of failed family
exchange. Weathered parent material out of reach,
surrendered to the geography of not being enough.
The legal aid solicitor thanked you for letting go.
Though it took the earth's orbit to realise
nothing can be taken from you
if you give it up willingly.

11.
Your son sends you a photo of a cat.
You send him a photo of a dog.
This is not a metaphor
nor the start of a conversation
where you breach the protocol
of distance. You can see his voice
and he can hear your stare.
Somewhere is not a place
a face can disappear
unless set as daily homework.
You make a joke over the phone
knowing it is not funny
to reassure a child that the world
is still around. Dad jokes only
work when nothing is at stake.
It's his birthday soon, he'll send
a picture of a cake and you will
send a picture of a candle.

12.
Taking a child to the domestic airport.
Check your ID as a legal carer at check-in,
an accomplice as unaccompanied minors line up.
Sit in the departure lounge waiting for
the absence to arrive, watching a small
figure being escorted by an affirming stranger
attending to their every need, the final meek
wave from the bend of time's tunnel as tides
of guilt and misplaced tears wash over.
They've lost the replica plane you gave them.
You've left your mobile at reception.
There is no way to say
how much went missing.

13.
All these selective memories. You begin
to experience resentment at being responsible
for another being. The economics of distance starts to
land, bruising the softness of seeing your only offspring.
Required to travel regularly interstate, staying together
on a foam mattress on your mother's spare room floor.
Unable to retrieve love from the deep end of a gene pool
sitting sullen at the bottom, a shiny pointed rock.
Their sleeping face is somehow foreign now,
reasonable requests sound like buzzing insects,
feeling numb and rigid when you hold them close.
At a nearby park, you watch them on the flying fox,
unsure of other kids and the gravity of the situation.
Green stains on worn shorts from the constant falls.
You have the same face when it comes to being seen.

14.
When you arrive for pick up
your son is hugging another man.
This was not part of the birth plan.
You let the optics wash over,
shout *hello* from the driver's seat
(emphasising both the 'hell' and the 'oh')
try to strike the sweet spot between
support and breaking the embrace.

He is a care navigator,
an invested third-party
omnipresent in all exchanges,
another adult in this lifelong game,
who texts you occasional bleak reviews
based on his views of your paternal skills
when you arrive later than he had planned.

When you arrive home go straight out the back,
build a small fire in the rusted pit,
feed a parental self-efficacy guide to the flames.

15.
It's Fathers Day again.
A parent-specific holiday if schedules allow.
You read somewhere that a child in America
is more likely to live with a pet than with a father.
You've shared custody of a child and a dog,
so you are a standard deviation from the mean.

You also read studies
(as single parents are expected to do)
that show fathers
who are involved with their kids
have better mental health, drink less,
report lower substance abuse.
You're involved with your child
yet have sometimes failed on three
of those three fronts.

In the consent order, it states no one
is to smoke within 100 metres of this child.
Healthy conflict involves keeping conflict
in the picture. Having moved closer, you now
live near a factory that is emission-intensive.
You still don't know how to roll your own.
Studies have yet to compare the effects
of passive aggression to passive smoking.

16.
It's incredible how little one can feel.
You receive a text from your ex stating
they will *endeavour* to respond to an email
about dates for the coming school term.
You remember a psychologist telling you
to treat all custodial interactions
as business transactions. To remove
emotions but keep receipts, not that there
is anything to return (nor return to).
Adopt an impersonal and politely curt tone
on the phone, setting the agenda
as efficient co-producing child managers should.

Reread the text and wonder
if this is two parents doing their utmost,
flinging brisk telecommunications,
investing little in each other
in their child's best interest.
You read the text several times, veer
between rage and administration, remind
yourself to keep records of each moment.
It's incredible how much one can feel.

17.
There's always a big hollow when they leave for the other home.
Regulating the senses takes a few days (more nights).
Crave drink or weed but it doesn't kill it, dissociate
divide the self into distinct parts, the mathematics
of father as a six-letter word forty-five percent of the time.
How does one ever maintain this full-time part-time role?
The aching jawline locked into the steel of it all.
Be glad it still hurts, chest clutched heavy in a hallway.
Wash teen smells from discarded towels and t-shirts.
Wipe down their desk so it becomes your desk.
Find strange drawings of a future without you in it,
a raft of mystery wrappers under the bed

where their resting child head
has left its young adult indent.

18.
You are dropping off your child for the final time.
Check they have everything.
Let them play a favourite song,
one you've heard eighteen times before.
There is no need to ask for directions.
Safety lock no longer engaged,
the catapult of time catches you unaware.
When they walk up the drive, fractured
childhoods pass in the rear view mirror,
as concrete as pulling away from gutter and kerb.

Last night you dreamt about receiving a call
requesting you come down to the station
to verify your son's identity. You offered
the officer memories, together and apart.
The dream police don't accept these as proof.
They show you a photo of who your son could be.
When you awake, they are free to choose their fate.

|We're going to get nailed|

Have you ever seen a footpath on fire?
No, because there's nothing to burn.

I know we're in the worst drought in white man history.

You think every tree is sacred?
Not the ones near the roads.

Don't get me wrong – we're not environmental bastards.
Our priorities are life, property [then environment ranks third].

For God's sake, maybe we just listen to those blokes
[and girls] out there on the front line.

You remove heavy metals from the ground
turn that into tabled dreams.

We've done everything we can to settle with that group.
Offering men sex for cigarettes. Mining welfare.

Don't forget, as settled Australians [as Europeans]
we're now living and working [and occupying] areas.

A coffee urn in the hall. Woolworths vouchers and gunja.
Health care, low morale, christening everyone Solomon.

The plume is getting all the way
[they say] to South America.

Sharing the good news on coal [our gift to a developing world]

[We can't] make The Australian fire-proof
[have we reached] the warning of the light.

If it burns, tax it. If it keeps burning, regulate it. And if it stops burning, subsidise it. I am sick of the government being in my life.

The millionaires and billionaires who chose to invest in Australia are those who most help the poor stay young.

Are we doing enough about so-called climate change? In my view, too much. CC is a bogey man. Should I start with my Thatcher quotes?

The upshot is that the cause of the fires is certainly man-made. Our great policy phantom – Christ. We're going to get nailed.

[This secret needs to be spread widely.]

Disconcerting tendencies

A key trait of diplomats is inclusiveness,
every dishonest mover knows this.
      Henry Kissinger is dead.
      Never a war he didn't adore.
'Credible military threats' can be subdued.
As a child, stick a fork in a neighbouring kid
      test the physical limits of skin,
      form unstable relations with civilians.
The formal peace process requires hostility.
A conventional killer loses if they do not kill
      a face can be easily removed,
      the unconstitutional takes longer.
Maybe another's humanitarian concern
will corner you in the middle of a crisis
      beat it away with incendiary fists,
      kiss the cold lips of their mothers.
Count tens of thousands on one hand,
value the elimination of firstborns
      show no moral restraint in foreign policy,
      protracted campaigns are an aphrodisiac.
Occupation is opaque in the absence of life.
A cowboy doesn't need to be courageous,
      exhaust these stupid militant animals
      making human shields from memory.
The destroying hour is near.
Don't take orders from a weakling,
      bomb anyone who stays
      or anything that moves.
Negotiate on the basis of possession,
true diplomacy is a blood technique
      extol the virtues of corpses
      enjoy this stellar career.

recline

openings can be challenging
where to sit everyone who has a chair named after them

opera chair from investment banking requires ergonomics
being chair of an arts org is both pleasure and responsibility

(chair now an object, now belonging to or associated with person)
not everyone can be given the name of a monarch

> I enter my name into a chair name generator
> it asks me what I currently do in life
> (I work in an office/I do not work in an office)
> how often I work out will assist in calculating a title
> whether I see infrastructure as big or small

there is an art to naming furniture, there is more at stake
than any newborn child due to levels of production

seeking visceral connection with consumers
everybody wants a throne, nobody dignifies a toilet

IKEA has the process down to a science
all have Scandinavian origins

> beds have Norwegian place names, seating Swedish ones
> in my next life I will return as a Stavanger queen ensemble
> I will be a port to strangers' dreams
> a berth for bodies, ferrying the traffic of pleasure boats
> paying tribute to cruise administration

no mentions of chairs were made in the bible
(the more you rely on a backrest, the more you tend to slump)

companies fund chairs as part of good corporate citizenship
(Jesus was not a good corporate citizen, he liked to stand up)

billionaire is padded soft beige eco-leather with vintage walnut
(just one in 10 ASX 200 chairmen is a woman)

> I sit in this lounge chair and watch the first season of shows
> I sit on this swivel chair and preside over search engines
> (look up things with a back and four legs that can't walk)
> dream of a chair to carry the day weight of dreaming
> I look up dream chair online and become two inches of foam

a well-endowed chair requires chutzpah
catbird seat is the best place to chew the ear off a president

as Ellen DeGeneres says *Leaning forward in your chair*
when someone is trying to squeeze behind you isn't enough

we will break down before the office chair, these bare ends
not built to comprehend how many of us there really are

> microplastics have been found lodged deep
> in the tissue of living people for the first time.
> there is increasing concern about hazards within us.
> we have each swallowed the equivalent
> of one hundred stackable chairs

our lungs are an auditorium of unsustainable applause.

Cystometrogram

I tell the latest urologist
the last one only saw me for two minutes
as she inserts a thin wire into my urethra,
making a joke about the perils of medical
speed dating, debates whether to describe
male genitals as paraphernalia or equipment,
telling me it's easier to stick tape around a nice
shaved vulva compared to a set of hairy balls.
I'm not sure when I'll see her next,
given her books are full until next year
and I'm soon to disappear again under general,
though accounts kindly promise to text before then.
She assures me it's best to keep one's specialists
monogamous, that intimacy is required to interpret
telescoped patterns of skin found on the walls
of a degenerate shaft, trace scars however light.
The nurse is cursing my tight tube
asks if I've ever been punched in the groin by a lover
then inserts a lubed finger from behind
whilst asking what plans I have for Christmas.
Carols are playing as the catheter connects
with my prostate, given it's still November
it's a prompt to buy baubles and increase
my daily bran intake. For the sake of urodynamics,
I am filled and then emptied
like a fish stranded in a bathtub
hooked by the tip, slack in their soaped hands.
There may be issues on the latest medication
with retrograde ejaculation, sexually there is nothing
I long to return to, the flow of time beyond
the permit of a new pill or orgasm reversed.

The kidney that was removed when I was seventeen
is still out there seeking sensations, ghosts of organs
past never mature into a functioning self,
the urologist says it's possible the frequency
of night visits are due to the reflux of its absence.
They tell me to redress and I redress,
to keep a diary noting when things burn.

We will meet again within the flexibility of induced sleep.
There is nothing scary, there is nothing yet concrete.
The next time I piss, I miss the bowl completely.

The Specimens on Crown Street

Being a public patient in a private hospital, elective surgery outsourced as waiting list reduction work. Looking out at the mountain mist, their website states that many rooms offer peaceful views of the ocean and surrounding escarpment. No one has left here and not gone to heaven. The intake officer asks my age before saying I'm still too young for the memory test but do I have any metal in my head. I'm put on a trolley bed and then taken down to the day room, awaiting ether's dome behind blue curtains. The implied carnage drifts in between small talk about shifts and an understaffed collective weight, who is eating what/when/who, and the supervisor so tense chasing signatures on a new laser safety edict (some surgeons have been going beyond the scope of the known) before ensuring there is sufficient skilled labour to populate the arteries and lesions of the Illawarra. The nurse-in-charge shouts that there is blood up and down the hall in solid red dots as if someone has been jumping on theatre waste with a pogo stick. Someone gets a mop, identifies the shoe not the blood. Hitting a buzzer, I am escorted down the now-clean hall, the attendant waits at the toilet door in case I try to escape. I'm taken into the room to be anaesthetised, they're asking me what I do for kicks as if my tattoos are a backstory. I awake hungry, stormy eyes watching the respite scene. You only receive the complimentary high tea if you've had a baby, a cystoscopy will only get you pre-packed cheese & crackers plus free ural satchels. Each room has 24-hour Foxtel access and shared views on the state of the world and the need for extra comfort. In the recovery wing post-procedure one of the ward nurses cries out for us all to come over to the fifth-floor window to look down on a woman below on Crown Street, who is in apparent distress taking a piss in the middle of the footpath. This nurse is flushed with excitement and soon everyone gathers around to point and mock pants around ankles, the sensation of someone else's shame in plain sight enough to induce laughter and running commentary about junkies and undesirables, the sights you see from heights of entitlement. I keep looking at the ocean as they conclude she's actually taking a shit, just as the lights turn red. There is a rich mother grinning ear to ear as if the shit is in her hands as a keepsake. The whole ward is full of itself enjoying the distance of class. Someone saw the woman's arse as if we're not already naked. The hospital's proud slogan is 'People caring for people', I feel privileged to bear witness to the limits of brochure's care. Soon I'll put my underwear back on, before joining the other specimens on the ground who know that getting by is not a spectacle for those born in private spaces, faces pressed up against the towered glass.

⁃ Intensifier ⁃

⁃ If you swim in clear water, you can give yourself the illusion of being in control. Recently there have been several shark sightings not far from me. One of the northern beaches has been closed a couple of times. An aerial news shot showed a lot of people in the water. Fear sells well from above. A mega great white was spotted amongst a shiver feeding off a whale carcass. The second time was triggered by capitalism, all that fresh Christmas flesh clustered tight in the shallows. Sharks are unsure of what a person is doing there. Statistically, you are more likely to die if a cow collapses on you in a field or by an errant champagne cork. Far more people have died at the hands of psychiatrists than have been killed by a catastrophic shark bite. Rarely do surfers call for a cull or a royal commission after someone is taken at the break – in the wake of such events, there is evident respect for the choice to inhabit a predator's habitat and an awareness of the inherent risks. Whereas psychiatry tends to bury fatal side effects in fine print and the line bait of coercive dependence mixed with profit. Sharks don't like to eat people. People like to eat people (and sharks). Big pharma is an apex predator more than a megalodon. One shared trait is that the parts of the brain related to feelings aren't developed enough to produce a smile.

⁃ Ways sharks are not like psychiatrists:

- numbers have been in sharp decline since the seventies
- their existence is scientifically meaningful
- they are precise and do not seek repeat business
- humanity is not on the menu

† Shark and human teeth are quite similar. It's just that ours are blunter, softer, more prone to erosion. At my dental check-up, they showed me close-ups of rivers of saliva and a multiplicity of fissures

caused by grinding in my sleep in pursuit of sleep. My jaw is a victim of day residue. Pre-ground teeth are yet to be stocked at Aldi. They inform me I'm right-handed as I brush more effectively on the left side. They seem pleased with the accuracy of their forensic evidence, not to mention the mounting adhesive restorations bill. They propose a deep clean, assuring me receding gums will later reattach. *We'll take the full journey with your teeth* is their parting words. We are now committed, their super care as reassuring as a stapled four-figure A4 receipt.

↑← Dentistry VS Psychiatry. Being in people's mouths versus being in people's heads. Psychiatrists = no expensive equipment or supplies. Still get to drill holes in people. Dentist = based on science and a love of soft drinks. Still get to have an intimate relationship with someone in a chair. Psychiatry is mainly a solo mind pursuit, dentistry is a team blood sport. Root canal versus pharmaceutical possession. Dentists talk as much as psychiatrists, but dentists make sure the patient can't talk back. Both focus on cosmetics and jaw tension. Their love child is an oral dream therapist.

↓ My local beach is a sheltered low-wave beach. Conditions can be hazardous and unpredictable. The mind is not patrolled by lifeguards here. I often think of drowning but equally of love, drifting across the horizon in search of tear-producing ducts.

[I'm aware of how writers often turn to analogies of the sea. For the past few years I have lived in an industrial port town, visiting the same stretch of coastline close to daily. Frequent swimming in a familiar analogy brings me no closer to the workings of nature.]

⁀ As a general precaution, swimming should be avoided for up to one day after heavy rainfall. Elevated levels of bacterial indicators are still detected at the beach. Anxiety and depression are also clinically on the rise if you only read the headlines. You can smell the sewerage plant; the sooty oystercatchers have disembarked from the rocks. Council has erected a cluster of three signs randomly above one part of the shoreline. There has been overflow and water testing may indicate that swimming or slow walking may be a health risk. Some flesh-eating E. coli is enamoured with human waste. I swim anyway, becoming visual stormwater, turbid drains entering turbid brain within minutes. The wind renegotiates the health direction, pointing people towards the road and passing joggers who may have possibly shit themselves straining for a personal best.

There are several potential sources of faecal contamination on the daily news updates but politicians can't be contained between twenty-five metres of temporary signage.

⁀ At the watermark one can find all forms of household items: plastic forks, straws, garbage bags, the suck head of a vacuum cleaner. The need to domesticate everything is forensically laid out. I like the beach after a storm, while there is still misty rain at hand, the only dog walkers are locals who weather the change around them. The urban runoff of strangers from school holidays is still present but no French Bulldogs, gentrification has taken a day off.

⁀ NO DOGS is painted in white caps lock on the ground three times in the lead-up to the council sign that states this is a dog beach.

– The black steel comes in and gives the sand its daily performance review.

– I ask myself questions my shrinks ask: what state am I in? Google Maps informs me I can't currently be located before the cartography of self drops its pin.

– I walk past the mood charts of seaweed, washed up on a mood board of sand.

– My new psychologist suggests I be mindful and choose a mantra to untie myself from the past. I whisper *adrift* repeatedly until it turns into an anchor.

– Give the youth anti-depressants before they're depressed. Fill every pill with salt water. Research the placebo effect of being told you are enough.

– Rough seas tend to form within some families.

– According to some 'experts', bipolar disorder can be inherited, knowingly passed down through the family like a bad debt. Diagnosed based on cluster consensus. I'm dubious about genetic factors but start to seek out the origin case having spent another summer swinging between seasons. My uncle seems to think it all comes down to one very enterprising woman on my mother's side who made infants' soft-soled shoes in her dining room. The premise is enticing, I think of Hemingway's unborn, the fixation and the florid compression of facts. Turns out she was an entrepreneur, becoming so successful she had to expand to an old bakery and employ extra labour, becoming the first building lit with electricity in the suburb. The family seemed to think she was fully manic as she was known for her generosity, apparently giving away her fortune to strangers. I looked up the DSM-V and generosity is yet to be listed as a criterion. When I was at university I took out a student loan to buy a non-crumpling tan cotton suit and took three different girlfriends to see Phantom of the Opera. I can't remember what I spent the rest on, I know I gave a lot of myself away. If this wasn't certifiable, the fact it's still being indexed annually alongside my loathing of musical theatre should be enough. How do you self-correct rapid currents in your head without the constraint of banks, waiting for impulse control to become less remote and rest in your own hands? I've walked on the roofs of parked cars, become Jesus of the Stars. I've stripped naked in public, full of accelerant and thoughts of transcendence. This constant fever. Theft has often been at the heart of it all too – small, sudden, done before consequences or cameras could be considered. It is one of the few times I feel truly calm, along with immersing myself in the sea.

~ Can a bipolar person truly love? I would argue we can, floridly, anything from a crest to an anchor.

ᛌ I don't subscribe to the phrase waves of loneliness. It's a cheap metaphor at best but at worst there is no collective experience of being alone. The ocean is where I feel most connected, immersed in the unrelenting pursuit of staying afloat.

~ The number of people participating in pharmaceutical re-creation each year is increasing.

– Things I don't want to be returned as: a nocturnal observer, a non-repeating prescription, a psychedelic melange.

– I believe that all psychiatrists are reincarnated as vertical blinds.

– I decided to re-patent myself as breakwater.

⁺ I drive to get supplies. My mechanic has informed me my car is worth less than my mobile phone. My new psychologist is big on balance, I'll tell them next session. At the shops, I experience a fugue state and arrive at the register with a trolley full of things I don't recognise. The assistant tries to scan me. I'm free to dissociate, I buy a kilo of salmon. All the fish's eyes are looking at me, full of sadness and ice.

⁺ I am awoken by the sound of a teeth grinder starting up, cutting through enamel at the front of a mouth. Anterior thoughts are the ones everyone sees when you don't smile, so it's important to keep them in excellent shape. I called the council of fractured sleep and lodged a complaint, asking them where the line is between suburban construction of the self and becoming a power tool. They inform me under new regulations head work may now occur at any time, as long as I permit it. Productivity is central to the economy. I report my loudest thoughts to the noise police. The cement mixer has been going all night, turning every fear concrete. They turned down my complaint, reassured I was alone and not irritating a sleeping partner. Tongue indentations are evidence of biting off more than I can chew, trying to reconcile the endless shifting night sights.

– Concrete thoughts: Bathers are brief. Anti-psychotics leave little to the imagination. There is no perfect rhyme for Diazepam. Time is the congress of the universe. Taxidermy is a dying profession.

↓ Witnesses say a group of people were standing on rocks near an area known as Hill 60 behind my son's new school when a large wave hit, knocking them into the surf overnight. A full-scale search of land, air and seas began around 10pm with the bodies of three men recovered from the water soon after. They were total strangers in the same location, caught off-guard together. The police said *[This is] just an absolutely horrible way to start the long weekend.* Meaning *Their fire went into the water, and there it was put out.* Choppers continued to circle the next day above the lookout 250m above sea level, above the sign that reads NEVER FLY BEHIND TAKE OFF POINT. The whole sky is also the whole sea and both are on pause. I dive in and swim in the bay below the next morning, in this body that held their bodies that now holds mine. This is rated the fifth most deadly fishing location in Australia I'm told by another local. It's hard to track a rogue wave down and charge it with a criminal offence. A current becomes a wanted criminal, the density of water willing accomplice.

↓ Flies gather on the eyes of a dead seagull, swept by the storm to sleep.

– The requiem sharks prepare a torpedo of song. I sing with them.

↓ Out of our depths, even our last breaths, we are never alone. I'm not sure if that's true but I listen to the blue and it's humming.

– Thalassophobia. A fear of deep bodies of water, a fear of that which seems vast, dark, dangerous. A photograph of a lake. Seeing the word 'sea'. A sinking feeling. Of what lies below the surface, the monsters we make or meet, malevolent seeing creatures. A fear of what is beneath fear is truly primal. No psychiatrists here, no teeth. I find a mantra ray saying:

If you let the ocean within you run wild, without any control, it will definitely control you.

Vision

The optometrist informs me
legally I shouldn't be driving
even though eye tests are not required
in the state of Queensland.

She asks me to look at her right ear.
She asks me to read the bottom line.
She asks me to roll back into my head.

The sales consultant suggests
given the shape of my jaw
length of face, a tendency to stare,
something square would best suit.

He tells me myopic people have high-strung dispositions.
He tells me he is given to moments of introspection
and is deeply fond of daydreaming.
Splashes his lenses with cold water on each break.

'What is your favourite colour?'
We sit at a white desk and I say *black*.
He asks what I do. I reply *Write*.
'An artist. So maybe something alternative?'
I ask exactly what that would look like and he says blue.
Offers up a generic blue frame that he owns too.
He's not into art or being difficult,
perhaps he peruses another planet's flightless sky.
An eagle's eyes fill most of its skull.
I just want to regain normal vision behind a wheel.

I will hold books further away.
I will coax my pupils daily to increase their focus.
I will turn the head as far to the left as possible,
keeping the rest of the body quite still.

An average optometrist earns $120K annually,
redirecting waves and dispensing bent light,
turning night to saline. This private company
turned over three billion last year, taking
federal handouts while we were blinkered
[having lost the ability to see a future].
A common theme of their UK adverts is a character
mistaking sunshine for an old flame, everyday objects
like the person you live with as a crumpled coat on the bed
[we recognise them as being the same size but ever distant].

I chose the pair the sales consultant recommended.
Money is an issue. I don't want to be difficult.
Sight's greatest spectacle is its unseen workforce.
The constant strain of commerce. Two-for-one
close-up magic, conjuring the illusion of options.
I can't read the small print without this new prescription.
The oscillation between oculist vs occultist,
the crumpled coat on the road vs a dead body
[knowledge of the measurable/knowledge of the hidden].

We assure ourselves night blindness will pass.
We assure ourselves the consequence is better blood flow.
We assure ourselves the vanishing point will follow.

The sales consultant shakes my hand.
Offers me free alcohol-free cleanser.
Gives me a glossy brochure for *Corporate Eye Care*
the class divide extending its frame of reference.
The script is written before we open our eyes.

Thumbsucker

I read a post on the local community notice board
letting everyone know to check their tyres
as kids have been going around Port Kembla
loosening nuts, you could be driving down the highway
doing 100km one morning, hot beverage at hand
thinking about the 'first sighting' of Keanu Reeves
as the founder of the Holy Roman Empire
when a front wheel comes off
[longevity is only acquired through acts of coronation].
Apparently, there is a higher incident rate near the pie shop
who have taken to writing warnings
on their blackboard next to that day's special beef crust
[if they named a pastry after Keanu
it would be called Thumbsucker
a sausage roll containing a battered baby frankfurter
where every bite tastes like echinacea.]
Everybody on the community thread is outraged,
no one's called the police.
No one has called Keanu despite his abiding love
of custom-built motorbikes and titular assassins
[who wouldn't call the cops either.]
Yesterday a car did a 20-metre burnout out front of my house
part of a Macedonian wedding party across the road.
They had their own traffic cones and a tightly strung band.
Some rituals have been passed down through the centuries.
The rubber smoke cloud covered relatives and bystanders alike
several of whom stood by their own cars smoking in unison
[some of them looked on like Neo, some jaded lean Constantines].
Everyone was suitably dressed, part of the regional steel town matrix.
Wheels are everything around here, from dart boards to prams
revved-up men becoming spare parts, sans custom-built Method 143

the ultimate American performance cruiser. A concept like freedom,
a cool breeze over the mountains or teens with an adjustable wrench
young blood with no sense of consequence, dropping out to pursue
running red lights, a few teeth lost to the mischief of their age
[cast in a role where they wake up, replicants of parents]
who when offered a choice of pills   will always take the blue one.

The Experience Economy

[Giving birth is a destination. Like a fair. Authorities are considering an admission fee before a couple even sets foot in pre-conception. At 'pre-contemplation'. Before the development of mechanical attractions. Charges for the ride – the carnival of carnal thought – remain free. Parents are then forced to stage a much better experience to attract guests, eagerly anticipating the start of the sensory festivities.]

[A combination of goods or services is needed. Sometimes the child requires immediate assembly, a time of teamwork and technical thrills. Other times they arrive via unpaid labour, the sweatshop of legacy and lust. This is what is called a productivity miracle. Placentas can be stored in an ice box to be re-gifted or on-sold as a luxury purse. This is one way we build close bonds with reproductive capitalism.]

[The labour experience is a perfect example — you're paying for so much more than a newborn. You're paying for the cosy ambiance. You're paying for skilled friendly staff, a superior birthing suite, a supportive cast of characters to spectate the big event online. The sensation of desire as existential demand, delivery as constant supply. The parent that gets recorded first on official record is considered the 'primary carer'. You can't copyright a face; some material is born into the public domain.]

[The first-born is often a non-fungible commodity. Facile sentimentality is the secret weapon of serial conception: one is often insufficient to trade, while two or more can form part of a set. They say subsequent ones are easier. Like saying the problem with water is that it breaks. The spectrum of choice is endless, from bath to bed to Uber, squatting in a space shuttle, an uncut umbilical cord unspooling through money and time.]

[The value of the transformation: they will soon have your eyes and consumer confidence. Walk down the compliment tunnel together: becoming patient too quickly *(applause)*, less consistent at night and more critical of morning *(muted claps)*, monitoring a child's whereabouts with an electronic device in the shape of an ankle *(rewards)*. Now is the time to relax, go to a nice restaurant and eat real food as a real couple, knowing where every item is on this menu.]

[An experience cannot lack the spontaneity of life: a nappy full of sudden sorrow; the discovery of back vomit; a bird hitting a window; walking in on your partner rearranging themself, deep in the consumption phenomena of pornographic daydream. While external problems may cause internal frustrations, we must offer fascinating displays of family, peacocks within the mundane. Needing ever more hardcore material is evident.]

[Pre-programmed experiences are pre-packaged and on-brand. Catchy slogans stick: *no kids are the new kids*. Tick. The child is just a prop for what's known as 'parentertainment'. A big screen shows a mother breastfeeding a clone. The playground swing breaks. A cafe opens down the road based on make-believe. Parents gather there child-free (but remain parents), talk about the joys of resentment-free raising, order empty cups of coffee and blank plates, paying for the magic state of gathering in our simulated connection environment.]

[Buyers of experiences are what Walt Disney termed 'guests'. Best guests attend kids' parties where parents neither make the birthday cake nor throw the princess-themed party. It's not even held at their home, an amorphous construct. The key to this business is staging a memorable event for the kids-in-us-all, whilst discreetly showcasing that ninety-percent of people with certified social mobility have self-confidence in turning children into stars. Mickey Mouse started out as a rabbit.]

[The provision of psychic gratification: divesting from dad, seeking better qualities of wife, the screened life immaculate, lying in bed with a lover now durational sleep companion. Parenting has only encountered trouble because we have failed to refresh our experiences, dethroned by the more traditional capacity of 'outcome' such as staying together and checking weekend weather apps. Our projected outlook will extend AI-fuelled family accessories, the interface with a surrogate life.]

[Parenting requires active participation. Name the child after another child or on-trend object, drive in an approved SUV, oversee endless summer sports, engage in engaged storytelling and intergenerational myth-making. If you're a venture capitalist, read an infant *Dune* at bedtime. If you're a stay-at-home parent, show them cavalier pictures of your cavoodle on Instagram. It's important to respect and preserve all forms of life, not unlike a modern CEO. Tell your child you are not like your parents. Services to your child will be intangible and occasionally memorable. A shared calendar with coloured squares will remind you who you planned to love.]

seaweed

we rarely swim together anymore
some days I try to force them in
but the chance of seaweed on their skin
is too much
                I ask them what it feels like
they say the texture is too great for words
unable or unwilling to create a cheap simile
for me to use in this public domain

jaffas

the even distribution of jaffas
during the previews
can be central to the fading sense of control
a parent has over their teen
once they are in the dark together

siege

walking up the stairs from Martin Place underground.
we had planned to go to the Lindt Cafe but a tantrum
about loose shoelaces waylaid plans for hot chocolate.
didn't fully take in early sirens or flashing blue lights
until I got texts soon after at the Museum of Sydney,
while we were building Lego skyscrapers without exits.
nearby parents frantically called their absent partners,
then the museum was locked down, all areas secured.
media began speculating wildly about multiple devices
all over harbour city, the views of an unknown enemy.
the less that was confirmed the more authorities knew.
it became about everyone outside, not the people within
while my son and I focused on the multi-coloured blocks,
unable to decide whether to make a shield or a rainbow.

stair/case
In response to George Karger's Duchamp Descending a Staircase *1946*

to cast myself on a wall
I literally had to stop time
let the staircase ascend my body
like a dream I had where I forgot
the idea of motion

I stand to strike blows for space
cast a shadow-like picture of
the plastic duration of desire
without trying to argue [post-coitus]
who is the child, who the last step

Sister

I don't think we ever met. There was sometimes talk of you at the neighbour's barbeque, in the silences where sausages burn and affairs begin. I once caught a glimpse of you in my mother, her frame wracked over the bathroom sink, sobbing until you came to be in the passing salt. My father never spoke of you or perhaps he did in his way, rearranging a child's room until it became his own, collecting newspapers in case there was mention of a girl missing, a photo of curls shaping a blurred face. The bones of small animals would turn up at the front door as if something was trying to form. Mum told me about you as an act of forced disclosure, another thing to hold underwater with my breath. As there was no death, there is no way to know if you were partial to flowers in your hair. Sometimes the night's air would take your voice, a phantom note full of a sibling's undelivered promise. There wasn't a backyard tree or shadow that didn't seek to hide you, the higher you climbed the less we looked. Some in this family have become unspoken, broken water no one wants to swim in. Those wet footprints where you walked into this house and shivered, waiting for us to hold the idea of more together. I never asked if you were delivered. An empty album without dates, words like *unborn* stored in the pockets of whispers. We buried our dog in the backyard that year, a shared grave with a small cross on top. Classically ghosts manifest because of other's unfinished business. The day I was told she didn't exist was the day I stopped digging.

Kale

In her arms she cradles the kale, knowing these are precious days. She stares down lovingly at the kale, who stares back. She's never sure if she should let others hold her kale, as it is young and delicate in unfamiliar hands. Closer in lineage to wild cabbage than polite strangers. At the farmer's market she shops wisely, putting root vegetables underneath her pram and a loaf of linseed bread on top. It's important to stay hardy, offspring thrive in wintertime. Her mother always tells her how she raised kale better in her day, even though kale did not exist back then. Day care is not an option, neither is leaving her kale in the car, the sun being what it is. She abhors those who describe their young as ornamentals. Her partner works away picking fruit. Some days they carry their silence as absence but things are often sweeter after a frost. She sends photos of their kale by phone—growing in the dirt, covered with lightweight fabric, gently tucked into its raised bed. She frets. She is not a good enough mother. Her friends reassure her she is the best mother this kale could ever hope to have. She still feels like she lives alone. There are few ways to fill the hungry gap.

a dog is not a child

    claiming a dog is a child
    is not a small claim.

seeking consent orders
rows over weekly visitation rights
the presumption of daily walks.
at what age can a pet speak for itself?

    few judges allow the argument that a companion
    animal is more than a short-lived emotional asset.
    quality time with three guinea pigs.
    equal access to a dead goldfish.

reports say Britney Spears is single again citing
irreconcilable difference, fights for fur babies
weighing up the merits of a gifted Doberman
the indeterminant age of an adopted Shepherd.

    constant change
    leads to defecation indoors following
    broken chains of command.

legal advice states canine equals property.
soft purchase of paws, these adopted jaws
registration papers chewed up in contempt.

    bumper sticker on passing station wagon reads
    Granddoggy On Board or *My Child Has Four Paws*.
    a cheetah strapped in a stroller, wolves with our eyes.

barking is an ineffective avenue of expression.
watching 'our' dog and it is still a 'dog'
head cocked to comprehend conditional love.

    no one is sure what's in a dog's best interest.
    sentient is not the same as *infant*
    anthropologists find a finite line between
    breeders and the experience of birth.

courts are an extension of the childhood home.
not all loving creatures can be amicable
social pack animals now thriving on their own

    we walk daily in partnership
    with the wild unknown.

Child Support [Calculator]

*If you do not know some of the other parent's details,
then the estimate will be incorrect.*

*If you do not know some of the other parent's care information,
then the estimate will be incorrect.*

*If you do not know how many children you want to support,
then the estimate will be incorrect.*

☐☐☐☐☐☐☐☐☐☐☐☐☐☐

*If you do not know the number of nights,
you might find the night estimator useful.*

*If you have any other dependent children,
declare them as a depreciating asset.*

*Self-employed parents are loopholes.
Only nurses and doctors can claim non-slip shoes.*

☐☐☐☐☐☐☐☐☐☐☐☐☐☐

*You can add up a 'child'.
A child is made up of 50% care and 50% cost.*

*Extracurricular activities can not be covered.
A pair of runners need to outlast the desire to run.*

*There may be a terminating event. If the child dies or becomes
a member of a couple you no longer have to pay child support.*

☐☐☐☐☐☐☐☐☐☐☐☐☐☐

This is not David/Acting as Saul.
This is where soul intersects with machine.

When circumstances change, split all costs into sounds.
This is a case being activated, this an account being closed.

Only contact us if you think this decision is correct.
It's easier to separate than it is to end this assessment.

☐☐☐☐☐☐☐☐☐☐☐☐☐☐

Prime Cuts

1.
swimming in the free ocean pool,
mind chattering
investment portfolio and *sweat equity*
swallowing trapped ocean water,
dead skin,
the distilled essence of developers.
The signs say not to push, jump, or bomb –
you talk underwater.
Those who swim outside the lanes
know what it's like to watch
others surge ahead,
cutting through the pool's skin
rising out of water like an interest rate.
The showers are hot (or lukewarm).
Bump into neighbours who inform you
they are retiring from work next week.
They bought before the viral boom
and you are roughly the same age.
Congratulate them.
Winter is close and this will soon all close.
Utilise the utilities, naked as an unpaid bill
knowing the season for debt is year-long.

2.
We touch the OUCH OUCH rock
daily or close enough.
It lies at the northern end of the dog beach,
in the corner of rock platforms
where my son says the wind and stuff shape us.

Every walk it is a brief touchstone
a turning back towards the south,
where childhood is impossible to remove,
a reminder that vicarious trauma is a tag
resistant as white spray paint.
Council has not painted over the graffiti.
On the way back we find
a pelican's head on the beach,
vertebrae exposed
a ladder to its final thought.

3.
I meet you for coffee and your other husband
arrives (you've double booked.)
We discuss aging, reduction of the body to complaint.
Your other husband recommends I get on the roids,
before hip tissues tear or I have a fleeting affair
with a local gym, says we're nearer seventy than thirty
get that testosterone swimming again.
We discuss having younger lovers (clichéd)
benefits of nerve flossing (peripheral)
the cost of health insurance (premium).
An ant drowns in my latte. A friend of yours
has died and it's chilly on the other side
of the window, watching everyone who passes.
You take photos of me posing with the cold cup.
Later when you text them through,
I see the seventy-year-old in me.
He doesn't seem to know what to do with the years.
I wonder what human growth hormone does to tears

(given it retains bodily fluids as muscle). I want to cry.
I'm training my tendons to form new attachments.

4.
The rescue kelpie up the back is tethered
permanently to a pole near their back door.
Animal welfare says as long as it has shelter
and is released for an hour daily, this is not
considered unreasonable restraint. The family
suffered a small child's death a few years back,
occasionally give voice to the wrenching event.
I offer to walk the dog, don't file a complaint.
They move out a few weeks later. A seizure
notice arrives in the mail, their companion is
set to be destroyed if fines remain unsettled.
They left without a forwarding address, soon
debt collectors appear at our front door
      chasing arrears that can't be paid back.

5.
At the rock pool in town,
a group of guys with a young goat
tied to a rope, blinking amongst the salt
and rock and spray. They'd named it George.
Sunbathers were posing with it for photos
– bikinis and thong meets beard and wattles -
to post online until they were told
it was being cooked in the coming days.
Though goats much prefer happy faces,
not everyone is smiling at George now.

(Un)found(ed)

1.
I have lots of family I adore in Texas.
Texas is extremely conservative.
I'm extremely conservative.
On every metric of gun ownership
we're generally friendly, boy-howdy types.

2.
Tibet. I want to know why
Buddha's ears are so long.
Organic mind farming. Fairtrade prayer.
Snow white yoga. It would be even better
if I could find a piece of Tibet in Europe.

3.
Italy has a big thing for me.
Maybe it's the pizza or maybe it's the gondola rides.
Definitely the gondola rides.
Gondola rides fascinate me.
I also like the pizza.

4.
I would go to the Garden of Eden
before Eve or Adam ate the apple.
Don't know how the apple got such a bad rap.
I would sleep with Adam, using the skin
of the snake as a condom.

5.
Australia. Many of our snakes are dangerous.
Now the law says we cannot kill them.

Now there are people in every suburb
living on mown grass, odds on snakes aren't.
You should be fine if you get a wet ankle bite.

6.
Norway. Dream baby dream.
Second happiest country in the world.
Newborns are soundly asleep outside.
Workers make their own pickled lunches.
Everyone has a seatbelt on in bed.

7.
Go somewhere safe like Antarctica.
Buy all the nappies now.
Don't buy pork rolls, they don't wash hands like we do.
Kissing is high risk, so are kids.
If you don't open your windows the virus can't get in.

8.
A room with a caged divider.
So there was no concern about safety and well-being.
I would say home, I would say cross the line.
I would ask myself if I was there.
I would not be there.

9.
Within the stomach of a celebrity chef.
Gizzi Erskine has a beautiful healthy gut.
Gordan Ramsey, Jamie Oliver, Nigella Lawson.
Even George Dimitrios Calombaris shits.
I'm really into gastronomy.

10.
Sadness is a garden between two walls.
Staycations still require attractions.
Taking a shower reminds us of the dirt.
I found myself in the corner of my eye.
You can't cheat on your loneliness.

Year of the Rat

My real estate
sent over a pest controller,
who dropped forty wax baits
via a hole to nest in the roof,
sealed them in with silicone caulk.

The agent assured me
I am a good parent/slash/tenant
unlike stressed rats who devour their children.

The agent suggested I see the baits
as a small reward for not asking for too much.
Given the cost of living,
a faulty gas oven and leaking toilet
can wait for the next inhabitant.
I don't want to attract their negative gear.
The constant fear is being aware of your rights.

Soon the scratching abates, all droppings disappear.
The real estate agent remains a permanent fixture.
Any means taken for rodent removal is,
as a rule, quickly discovered by the rats;
if not, the terror alone engendered
by the ever-diminishing tribe,
is sufficient cause for them to flee,
the mysterious legislative powers that haunt us.

Reserves

As governor of the Reserve Bank
*Rents will only start to fall
once people form bigger households.*
Consider bringing in a flatmate.
Eight warm bodies can be added to any room.
Convert that hatchback to a studio apartment.
We need more on average to live in each dwelling.
Squeezing into a rental pathway is getting tight.
Tents are at a premium, breaches in high demand.
That's the price mechanism at work.
To deconstruct a dwelling, see a hole in the floor
as another door, move your growing son
into the living room, sub-let their bright future.
The housing sector sits in the economy of the heart.
Other options – never leave work or stay at home
with ageing parents until someone retires from life.
In general, other animals do not fear their dead,
a severed head will not deter occupancy.
*We need that level of locked-in commitment.
We need people to help us bring this balloon down.*

Landlords

Prospective tenants can be so hurtful.
Where's the rest of the hall?
Do you mean that mirror is the window?
That wall is placed too close to this wall.
Small flats are made for small people.
There is comfort to be found in constraint.
Don't people get that?
How sensitive we are to scale, riding the sharing
economy wave, renting our homes out by the hour.
We're responsive to the strong rebound in demand.
Just have a look at our assets like you're a guest.
It is important to have very strict tenant selection,
a single mother will invariably increase their litter
single incomes suggest a lack of social integration,
a disability may lead to pre-fabricated arrears.
It pleases us when a tenant's aesthetic matches our own.
Cash in a white envelope ensures we are equals.
An unkempt duplex reflects directly on you,
we get a direct sense of your libertarian lifestyle
when there are issues with the sewerage system.

Behind these housing statistics are consequences,
there is nothing we can do about that.

Review

Real estate agent sends me a new lease || with a larger increase than prior years || I suggest a halfway place || where we can meet in the middle || of their increased costs || servicing a Lexus || branded gym gear || and my decreasing faith || in secure future housing || the outsourcing of angels || the lease has both landlords listed || investment couple || so I look them up online || they're on a podcast || talking about buying 9 properties || in 15 months || in that same period || I ate approximately 51 Coles croissants || have much gravitas to show for it || one of their websites is about building empires || selling things people want to buy || like ads for clients || anything platinum || conceptual coins || and the biggest life lessons || that it's not easy to turnaround a cruise ship || that there's a good reason || niche rhymes with rich || which it doesn't || but who am I to correct || he provides off-shore staffing solutions || I find a post of theirs on socials || about passing government taxes onto tenants || which makes it sound like a baton || as if we're in the same race || as if we're both really living || under the same roof || and I will get to cross the line || between us || their main childhood recollection || seems to be about imported products || lessons learnt in their twenties || that a party is all about the numbers || and money never gets old || I am getting older || prefer small gatherings || the main thing I learnt in my twenties || is that people like them || will always take the last beer || from your fridge

Fifteen ways to be erased
Co-written with Saul Stavanger. Text in square brackets are Saul.

'Our school rejects that all forms of bullying behaviours exist'

1.
We spend up to three years of our lives in the toilet. I was thirteen when I first started regularly hiding in them. I would make sure no one saw me enter and then pick the stall furthest from the door as long as it was clean (or clean enough), drawing my feet up on the closed seat, tucked tight so no teachers could sight legs during a sweeping check.

Toilets offer solace in ways some people find in an emptied church – a chorused silence, the metaphysical self disrobed, prayers formed from necessity and pursuit. By this stage the bullying had reached a level that led me to frequently vanish, in flux between domestic tensions and the hypervigilance of school, unsure as to what lay halfway but also knowing it was safer to be nowhere than either.

Bully*: third-person present.
Bully*: noun; corned beef.
Bully*: harasser of the weak; harasser of the week.
*If you write the word *bully* three times during this recollection, they will reappear in your bathroom mirror.

2.
[Physically hiding is my first form of hiding: things like bathrooms, cubicles, and outside of PE block are the kinds of places I can sit away from everyone else. Talking to teachers to avoid going out to lunch, taking different routes getting home to avoid certain people and situations. I first started hiding in Year 3, when I was eight. I used to hide up in the library. It was the only place in the school that had air-con.]

[My first mental hiding was books – fantasy books. I read a lot of books. That worked for a while until kids saw I had books on me, which worsened the bullying. Books in breaks solidified that I was a weirdo, an outsider.]

[I began world-building little towns, then cities, then made a country – the map was pretty terrible. Any free time I would dedicate to daydreaming or writing down any little or important events and timelines from this fictional universe when I couldn't talk to many people in my class. Created my first world – it had the illusion of a real world where I could hide. I didn't exist in these worlds, I just watched over them and decided what happened. School was a place where I couldn't be me.]

3.
Hi ▇▇▇

We are still not sure if we will take things further with the police. Unfortunately, outside of CCTV footage, there are no witnesses to the events.

I want to say how terribly sorry I am that this has happened to Saul.

I have every confidence that the school will deal with these boys seriously once they have been identified. However, I do think you should consider ▇▇▇▇'s suggestion that this be taken further with the police.

Which books did he lose?

Does he have any friends?

I hope this does not cause his social development to regress and his anxiety to increase.

Kind regards,

Learning Support

4.
I – and now my son Saul – have attended multiple schools due to bullying. Perhaps the education system hasn't really changed that much in thirty years. We are both experts at hiding, though theirs is more refined than mine. I read in the local paper that their previous high school has recently been part of a trial of school 'wellness' workshops where boys paint each other's fingernails while being taught about toxic masculinity, discussing self-harm and what it means to be a man. I think of the way my son bit their nails down to the skin while they were at that school, eating themself in front of me. The aim is for young blokes to see it's just paint. The same way we tell young kids it's just blood. Some parents have apparently slammed it as nutty and weird. I see them painting their children into a corner, and once cornered those kids see red instead of stop.

5.
[Sometimes I would go and watch a bird's nest in the grounds. I would go there to both hide and read – and I liked the birds. One day some kids tried to smash the bird's eggs and I tried to stop them and my opinion didn't really matter to them at all. My opinion never mattered.]

6.
I looked up reviews of Saul's last school on Google. Someone with the handle 'Jesus Sparklez' has written, 'If you wish the unhappiest education for your child. This is the place to go.' A better motto than the trinity of text nailed to the school's front gate: RESPECT × RESPONSIBILITY × INTEGRITY. It's a conceptual commitment at best. When my son was surrounded by dozens of students, being called a *faggot* after their 'friend' announced to the whole cohort that Saul identified as pansexual, the new guidance counsellor spoke at length about the school's supportive culture for queer kids and avoided the F-word in case saying it would manifest a faggot before him. Like to see that guidance counsellor de-escalate a fist at the point it regrades a face. Like to know the last time someone reduced him to a noun.

7.
[First time I was physically in danger,
I was walking home and one of my main bullies
started tailing me on his bike.]

[When we got back my bag it was turned
inside out
and my stuff was all over a field.]

8.
When Saul was assaulted walking to the station and on the train getting home from one school, the learning support team suggested they arrive and leave before the bells as they couldn't guarantee their safety. They don't even have bells anymore (whoever created the end-of-days mixtape, with its over-reliance on Alice Cooper, needs to know that school's never out for many kids.) We were told to go to the police; we were told Saul was sensitive and provocative. Adjectives

are positioned to undermine victims (even the term 'victim' has an unspoken narrative of responsibility in schools, as if children assign themselves that role.)

Saul started arriving at different times and entering the grounds covertly from a back path, their actions the result of education as a public institution, minimising harm to itself. One morning they turned up to walk this path and smelt decay nearby, turned to see the carcass of a juvenile whale rotting on a reef off the beach at the end of their school's street. Onlookers gathered, keen to see the shark feeding frenzy. It's one of the first memories that springs to mind whenever we pass by their former school gate.

We withdrew Saul from that school the following month, towing them out into deeper water so they could float, leaving all the detritus of that year in the shallows.

9.
Saul and I watch *High Fidelity* and the next morning, knowing their love of lists and rating things, I ask for their Top Five* bullies:

1. [███ o. Would attack me on the train. Spreading rumours. YR8]
2. [██ n. What didn't she do. Told me to kill myself multiple times. YR8]
3. [█a█. Punched me in the face and started the homophobia stuff. YR7]
4. [█c██. Chased me home on a bike. YR5]
5. [██ b. The taser person. YR3]

[*hard as there are quite a few, I can't remember all their names] I hear this as 'games'.

[The school counsellor advised me to ignore the name calling and it would go away—they were just nicknames. Sitting in a white room, low chromatic, at a wooden desk with a black chair. She didn't really listen—there is a certain way they speak that tells you they're not listening, offering the same advice as last time.]

10.
Hesitation marks appeared in the margins of my son's learning. They began to doubt words, even when they were written down or bolded in emails or on their own lips, shedding trust in language and that adults are licensed to name things as solid or known. Every adult, from year advisors to learning units to teachers to relatives to parents, became unreliable when they opened their mouths. Often I felt I had nothing concrete to offer beyond our shared doubt.

11.
[I moved interstate. There was no bullying at my new school at first. I thought things were going to be great. Once my one friend left, it felt like no one wanted to be associated with me at all. Playing a game of tag, I was hiding behind a tree because I'm not a fast runner. These kids from the year above started making fun of me for being socially awkward (the teacher's phrase) and I cried. They grabbed my bag and took it into the toilets and threw it in the urinal. All my work was in it. Classwork, books, my world-building. Drenched. Ruined. Went and found a teacher and I got detention.]

12.
I bump into a friend while taking my dog (and my doubts that I have anything meaningful to write about bullying) for a walk. She says 'Perfect – doubt is what bullying is all about.' All the ways it centres and amplifies doubt. Doubt of your child's take, their muscle memory and their written account. Doubt about encouraging your child to be empathetic towards the bully, doubt that the bully truly exists. Doubt that the school has it under control, doubt that they're taking it seriously, doubt that they have the mechanisms to manage what's happening out of their sight. Questioning where responsibility lies, who's telling the truth, the possibility that your child is somehow soft or you're not hard enough or you're both too sensitive – the 's' word again, lodging itself in your subconscious as various non-parents recommend self-esteem tutorials or martial arts classes. For both of you.

One day, one of Saul's main antagonists said he had a taser in his bag and was going to use it on Saul. The school's response was to doubt that there was a taser or that the word 'taser' had been used. I wanted to obtain a stun gun after this. And use it on the other kid's parents. Who are probably full of another form of the same misplaced rage as I am. Not many parents talk about the violent fantasies that can play out after your own child is directly threatened or harmed. Stunning to look into the light of your child and see yourself burning.

13.
[Year 6 was really bad socially—isolating and kids making bad rumours about me, special rules for me to not be able to play handball, pushing me out the back. It was my only way to hang with other kids. I was very depressed. I felt suicidal, holding myself hostage under a desk with a knife to my wrist.]

[The most significant out of all the things people don't tell you about bullying is that being resilient doesn't solve the problem. When you're told that you're super resilient, it has the same effect as being told to ignore it and it'll go away. No matter how emotionally strong you are, having every aspect of your identity mauled by your peers will hurt.]

14.
You know there is no good–bad binary here: one of Saul's long-term bullies turned out to have a mother dying of cancer, another was experiencing regular beatings at home. In some ways, their victims were the most reliable intimacy they had in their lives, often one in which they had a sense of agency and control. The word 'bully' likely evolved in the mid-sixteenth century from the Middle Dutch word *boele*, which loosely translates as 'lover'. A term of endearment, a familiar form of address to an intimate friend. Often a bully is the first people we are pursued by, the first people to make meaningful physical contact, the first to give us pet names, the first to fixate and to seek us out in times of shared confusion and doubt.

15.
[Bullying is a sea of faces, morphing and changing. Its only desire to consume lest it devour itself. Although it is always in a state of flux, it hates change, even more so difference, covering it with the oozing sludge of its toxicity. It is infectious and can transform even those who don't want to be consumed by it, while the fate of those who refuse to give in isn't much better—the sea of faces inspects every part of them and tears each one to pieces. The monster cannot be destroyed, as its faces are always changing.]

Coda

My son's advisor called me as I missed parent–teacher night. Fortunately, their latest school is a move away from 'appointment learning'. Their motto is *One student at a time, in a community of learners*. Teachers are advisors, parents are peripheral planets, students are agents of their own making. I still have a vigilance around school calls, built up through years of Saul being bullied or retaliating to bullying or being attacked and preparing myself to legally represent them. But this call was to tell me how Saul is thriving, how they lead the class discussions, how the world-building project they're working on is blowing minds, how Saul spends their time beta-testing friends' game designs and playing Catan in beanbags, that there is funding to support all the autism spectrum disorder kids in ways that can be defined by the kids themselves.

Saul hasn't been called a faggot or a retard this year. Hasn't been hit or kicked or spat on or told to kill themself. No bags emptied or books stolen. Catches public transport again. Wants to stay at their mum's on school nights so they can catch even more trains. New records. The faces don't appear so much in sleep now*, the night terrors have finally stopped and there are soft reports that their dreams are slowly becoming their own.

*

[Among the sea of people I spot the amorphous creature again. A colossal tide of echoing laughter washes over me, knowing it has already gotten the best of me.]

In the lead-up to Christmas, I take Saul to a foragers' market in the same suburb as their previous high school to find some final gifts.

Saul's hesitant to go, given the geographic association and the potential hypervigilance they may need to negotiate. I reassure them that all that was twelve months ago and they are safe with me. Saul isn't safe with me. While looking at handmade soap, I don't see Saul stiffen, face stripped of its natural colour. Saul comes up close, whispering in an agitated state that the bullies are over there but I'm not to look, *please don't look*. I look.

[I anticipate something happening and in fact hope for it so that this burning tension droning on in my brain will stop.]

Standing in a small, broken circle are Saul's past tormentors, openly mocking them across the stalls. Spoilt coal-coast kids, cruel mouths full of sweets. I hold the bath bomb in my hand tighter and stare back, as if a stare can dissolve their essential nature. Saul wants to leave but I keep staring, fixed on a target that's not on my back. I buy a pomegranate bath bomb. Nothing explodes. We leave together and we walk away alone, unsure how to transcend this.

[I do not remember the time it took or how long he said it would take, I just remember it being an eternity to me.]

Dad/Bingo

d	a	d	d	y
bread/ winner	prog-rock (prog-enitor)	rivet (ing)	lord lion	bear(d) oil
ah-fret/ he-fart	oak nurse	raise carnations	soft bod(e)	estranged sire (deserting arse)
step service	pizza dada	☻	one egg led to another	chromo zone
life-sized cutout	research product	muscle monitor	ambitious tools	Jack Torrance
talk about bastards	summit patriarch	Cronus clock	begets a child (forgets a bagel)	reminds everyone of death

A boy walks between his parents holding both their hands.
We cannot see their faces only his, full of confused wonder
and dread but not joy, a boy in between two adults can not
carry such possibilities alone. He is wearing the same outfit
he wore the day they parted ways, just before he was four
and old enough to stand on one foot for more than nine seconds.
He cannot recall walking without them or with them.
Their faces are too far away to say if they are still faces.
They are not walking towards anything, though things are moving,
passing by like a first front tooth or lying together on an unmade bed.
In his head, he is holding their hands but in this moment they
are holding him, the way passing clouds contain passing rain.
This image will let go, and their collective sky will not clear for years
no matter what weather the boy holds, in his head or with his hands.

Grounds for Divorce

No matter how kindly
you touch me, enter me
separation begins in the head
Barbara Giles

D.
After a few weeks of married life, her husband
preferred football matches to her pretty face.
She vowed that if she ever married again
her second husband would not be a football 'fan'.

I.
A Hungarian Civil Servant told a Judge
that he was being starved to death by his wife.
'She is a disciple of a nature doctor and refuses
to give me anything but raw vegetables.'
He obtained his divorce
– and immediately afterwards –
a good meal.

V.
When the only child of the union was
four months old, the father announced his
intention of hypnotising the baby.
The baby was to be put into a trance,
and in this state buried for four weeks in a tin box.
When the month had elapsed
the baby was to be awakened, hypnotised,
and buried again. They gave her a
divorce and custody of their baby.

O.
Equally strange was the successful
plea of Mrs. Helen Orwin of Des Moines,
Iowa, who complained that her husband
refused to remove his hat at the breakfast
table, and Mrs. Ruth Baldworth, whose
husband had one bad habit –
putting mice in her bed.

The Californian Courts
followed these examples very closely
by granting a divorce to Air. C. Christenson
because his wife served him with hot
asparagus, whereas he liked it cold.

R.
Mrs. Alice Burgess, of Chicago, had a
jolly husband. He was so jolly that
he told the same four jokes to his wife
at every meal, and on all occasions when
visitors called. The four family jokes
became a nightmare for Mrs. Burgess. She
even dreamed of them and appealed to
a lawyer. Judge Sabath listened to her
version of the jokes, was not amused,
and granted her a decree.

C.
In Idaho of late a wife of that region sought
a bill of divorcement, one part of her indictment
being that her husband smoked a pipe
in their bedroom. In his defence he
declared that he smoked only the best
tobacco, that his wife knew he smoked when
he married her, and might rationally have
expected the occasional fumigation of their
dormitory. He declared also that he habitually
smoked on the doorstep except when it rained,
and that his wife objected to his going to
the saloon when it did; as to his smoking in
the parlour, he agreed that it be tried once in
his early conjugal days, and had no inclination
to repeat the experiment. He was, therefore
forced to take occasional refuge in the bedroom,
but generally smoked out of the window,
as a loving and considerate husband should do.

E.
A North German spouse
sought release from a brute of a husband
because he advised her to go to the masquerade
as a captive balloon,
with a string tied around her ankle.

D.
In South East Queensland an unemployed couple,
whose main asset was a young child, drifted apart
in pursuit of visions that did not involve the other.
The mother was the primary carer of her interests
the father was in the middle of another single life.
Lawyers were not involved beyond these failings.
It was unnecessary for them to joust over
invisible things that could not be divided.
To chart the decline further is to void each heart.
They were more viable apart, the child is their forever.

Game

No one is clear as to when the deer first appeared.
Mistaking synthetic grass for snow,
shining diamonds in the darkness
disturbed by human nocturnals.
Once found in the escarpment of dusk
now running riot on residential garden,
a seasonal gestation of long robust legs.
Symbols of spiritual authority, dream regeneration
casting off wet antlers, velveteen lovers
lying in wait, game for another dominant rut
[we can appreciate the folk horror of it all.]

Since the turn of the century members have surged.
Faster than the birth rates of hunters, fallow and red
from sambar to chital to rusa, sightings of rare hog
quickly catching up with cane toads,
the insurmountable debts of rabbits.
Continuing their deep march into suburbia,
responding to the roar of grazing pressures
feral coryphée prancing outside bedroom window,
soft-launching themselves in nearby playgrounds,
dewclaw prints devilled on doorsteps, crowns erect
reaching beyond the conceit of the body.

There's much debate about how to tackle feral deer,
animals with eyes on the sides of their heads
reluctant to come under professional observation.
Culling efforts taken beyond the boundary of land
–aerial shooting, humane stalking, bulk ammunition
the control tools of regulation and reports cannot abate
these antlered interlopers, breaking every known curfew,

ranging in packs led by big bucks who dropped out
of the wilderness, without the ambition to graduate
to farming or plate, CCTV ghosts crashing through
pool fences and the false sense of order we cultivate.

A Port Macquarie resident was first charged
then stomped on in their front yard
fracturing bones, the fragility of coexistence.
The alleged perpetrator was a bull hart,
large-horned, the victim stated it stood up,
pointed directly at him with keratin splits,
made the clarion call of a coming civil war
before ghosting into the sacrifice of scrub.
Rail collisions are also common,
at the point of train-deer impact
driver regresses to bambi state,
fur becomes blood becomes track.
Their willingness to compete for pasture,
reducing sheep meat production,
breaking across borders with hard-hooved intent.

Red deer are rutting on a war footing
mounting new territories with pagan flesh
forming leks with uncanny vigilance,
celebrating the agricultural impact of breeding,
a lack of natural predators,
the complexities of sustained colonisation,
free from the constraints of monogamy.
Heat maps show them in the heart of CBDs,
a gathering menace in empty malls, roaming
major highways before dawn, cloven thumbs out

transforming car bonnets into crumpled steam
piquing the curiosity of panel beaters,
stemming the population growth of hatchbacks,
confronting motorists with their softening childhoods.

Nothing can stop them from moving through
greenish summer gold to winter's vivid blues,
mobile in ways we cannot wheel, feeling their way
into fringes of days, vexing us with thunder moons.
Corsican witch meat, reforming the fauna of worlds.

Kill [All The Birds]

the noise causes ear cancer
at the very least auditory hair cell loss
increases the mortality of feathers
diverts the flyways of gulls and terns
creating avian graveyards
[birds are public animals of capitalism]
these farms that span whole sea fields
that won't work as a breeze lacks accuracy
or representativeness [I'm no expert but]
the bureau doesn't seem to know a lot about wind

truth is, turbines complicate property enjoyment
they will be highly visible
like retirees at auctions
eyewitness accounts state they shrink the horizon
decreasing the value of a holiday house
limiting grand-children's selfies
ruining the beautiful view
[the visual impact is of particular interest]
the industrialisation of oceans
damages local cafe ecosystems
disrupting great southern males migration sites

it's sending the cetaceans crazy
shortening their exalted plume
separating mothers from calves
disorientating dolphins
colliding with dream catchers
altering cocaine shipping routes
now the fish have tinnitus
they can't hear their fins

swimming circles in benthic habitats
disturbing underwater cultural heritage
they're finding congenital malformations
in mermaids, the unmaking of the sea's bed

it's a blight on our coastline
these windmills aren't real movement
we are the citizens clear skies network
[chanting 'physical presence' at online protests]
we fear these acoustic engineers
calling upon stray electricity
didn't move to this pristine leisure environment
to be looking out at the future
got to give our heirs something to own
we don't want to make sacrifices
be made disciples of air currents

[even when streamlined
truth is an elusive creature]

Montage
written with an eye towards production

Sitting alone, David is blowing up latex party balloons. One of them explodes in his face.

David is making nachos with much pizazz, there is melted cheese stuck in his beard (employ a variety of lenses), which he combs in with greasy fingers.

It's night. David stands at the end of his son's smiling (real-time rendering). He gently kisses the sleeping forehead of another child.

Waiting outside the school gate, David takes the plates off the car and offers them to a more reliable narrator. Saul appears as a collage in the side window. As they pull away from this education site, the future is luminous (audacious premise).

At the cinema, all the seats are reserved for Yorgos Lanthimos and Nathan Fielder. The glowing EXIT sign is above the screen. David and Saul depart with credits (cross-fade to their popcorned silhouette).

On the phone, we see David gesticulating while holding spaghetti strands that intertwine storylines. His face is becoming a tomato (cut to a tomato).

Saul is throwing a frisbee and it removes David's head and both heads laugh together like seagulls (canted beach angle).

An asteroid hits Saul's desk (high-contrast lighting). They slowly enter the crater. It's an elaborate set.

David shouts orders from another room; Saul looms over the TV like every Nicolas Cage. Both have a predilection for symmetry.

(Classic docu-fiction). They are walking a kite and they are tied to a dog and the wind is a post-war newsreel.

At the gym. David is at the concept curl machine, sweating profusely, Saul is on the rowing machine and the fish eye circles. Nearby Emma Stone is climbing faux rocks.

Saul pegs silver nitrate film and socks on the back line while processing leaving home. The parenthetical: staying causes a pair of black jeans to burst into flames spontaneously (discordant strings).

David is holding the compression of time. Both hands are closed and open. Stills are spilling from his mouth (positive and negative.) There are no other props or cast nearby.

Notes

|We're going to get nailed|
This poem is built on a combination of direct and repurposed quotes from Barnaby Joyce, Andrew 'Twiggy' Forrest, Gina Rinehart, and various ABC News TV anchors.

(Un)found(ed)
This poem draws on found/unfounded online Quora travel threads.

Reserves
The italicised lines in this poem are direct and repurposed quotes from the former Governor of the Reserve Bank, Phillip Lowe.

fifteen ways to be erased
This was co-written with my son Saul Stavanger. The sections in square brackets are by Saul Stavanger; the non-bracketed sections are by David Stavanger.

Grounds for Divorce
This poem (in most part) is based on found text from a range of satirical columns via Trove:
D. Excerpt from 'Flimsy Excuses', *Newcastle Morning Herald and Miners' Advocate* (NSW), 28 May 1930 (P11).
I. Excerpt from 'Flimsy Excuses', *North-Eastern Courier* (WA), 12 July 1930 (P4).
V. Excerpt from 'Queer Grounds for Divorce', *The Register News-Pictorial* (SA), 7 February 1931 (P11).
O. Excerpt from 'Divorce Comedies', *Westralian Worker* (WA), 15 August 1930 (P13).
    Excerpt from 'Flimsy Excuses', *Newcastle Morning Herald and Miners' Advocate* (NSW), 28 May 1930 (Page 11).
R. Excerpt from 'Queer Divorce Pleas', *Queensland Times* (QLD), 14 May 1930 (P 10).

C. Excerpt from 'No Ground for Divorce', Western Mail (WA), 10 December 1897 (P 35).
E. Excerpt from life.

Kill [All The Birds]
This poem was written in response to information shared on community pages about the planned Illawarra offshore wind farms.

Acknowledgements

The Chess Game first appeared on Red Room Poetry commissioned as part of the *Punch Lines: Poets Play Duchamp*, 2019

I've been thinking about your birth lately first appeared in *Westerly 69.1*, 2024

|We're going to get nailed| first appeared in *Westerly Online* commissioned for Perth Festival, 2020

recline first appeared in and was commissioned for *Cordite: No Theme*, 2023; and *Best of Australian Poems 2023* (Australian Poetry).

The Specimens on Crown Street first appeared in *Rabbit: MUTINY*, 2024

Intensifier first appeared in and was commissioned for *Griffith Review 72: States of Mind*, 2021

Vision first appeared in *Australian Poetry Anthology 11*, 2024

Thumbsucker first appeared in *Hello Keanu!*, 2024

the experience economy first appeared in *Newcastle Poetry Prize Anthology*, 2024

Stair/Case first appeared on Red Room Poetry commissioned as part of the *Punch Lines: Poets Play Duchamp*, 2019

Sister first appeared in *Meanjin Autumn Issue*, 2025.

Kale first appeared in *Griffith Review 86: Leaps of Faith*, 2024

Review first appeared in *Industrial Estate* (Subbed In), 2024.

Fifteen ways to be erased first appeared in and was commissioned for *Griffith Review 75: Learning Curves*, 2022

This collection was written in Port Kembla on Wodi Wodi Dharawal land. Always was, always will be.

Thanks to Terri-ann for her unwavering support of my work, and for making room to put this collection out through her Upswell Publishing imprint.

Much gratitude to the funding support I received from both Create NSW and Wollongong City Council to create this work. Some of these poems were also written during my 2023 Poetry Flagship Fellowship at Varuna, to whom I am also grateful.

Thanks to my close readers and peers Felicity Plunkett, Jennifer Compton, Laura Jean McKay, Lucy Nelson, Mary Anne Butler, and Pascalle Burton for their invaluable time, insights and direct feedback (much of which made this work stronger and pushed me beyond the lines.) Jen – thank you for the deep dive phone exchanges.

To Lucy, your belief in my ability to write (and love) on through it all means the world.

To Saul, this book would not exist without you. Thanks for choosing to be my son, you are magnificent.

About Upswell

Upswell Publishing was established in 2021 by Terri-ann White as a not-for-profit press. A perceived gap in the market for distinctive literary works in fiction, poetry and narrative non-fiction was the motivation. In her years as a bookseller, writer and then publisher, Terri-ann has maintained a watch on literary books and the way they insinuate themselves into a cultural space and are then located within our literary and cultural inheritance. She is interested in making books to last: books with the potential to still be noticed, and noted, after decades and thus be ripe to influence new literary histories.

About this typeface

Book designer Becky Chilcott chose Foundry Origin not only as a strong, carefully considered, and dependable typeface, but also to honour her late friend and mentor, type designer Freda Sack, who oversaw the project. Designed by Freda's long-standing colleague, Stuart de Rozario, much like Upswell Publishing, Foundry Origin was created out of the desire to say something new.

www.ingramcontent.com/pod-product-compliance
Ingram Content Group UK Ltd.
Pitfield, Milton Keynes, MK11 3LW, UK
UKHW030827310325
5233UKWH00028B/186